The Most Important Lessons in Life

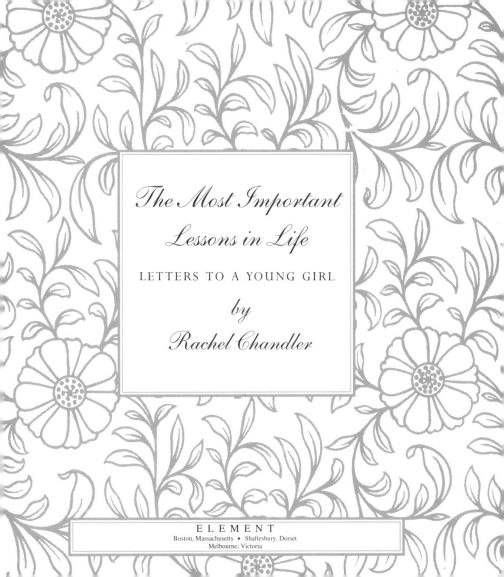

The Most Important Lessons in Life

LETTERS TO A YOUNG GIRL

by

Rachel Chandler

ELEMENT
Boston, Massachusetts • Shaftesbury, Dorset
Melbourne, Victoria

© Rachel Chandler 1998

Produced in cooperation with GuildAmerica® Books,
an imprint and registered trademark of Doubleday Direct, Inc.,
Box GB, 401 Franklin Avenue, Garden City, New York 11530.

Published in the USA in 1998 by
Element Books, Inc.
160 North Washington Street
Boston, Massachusetts 02114

Published in the UK in 1998 by
Element Books Limited
Shaftesbury, Dorset SP7 8BP

Published in Australia in 1998 by
Element Books and distributed by
Penguin Australia Limited
487 Maroondah Highway, Ringwood, Victoria 3134

British Library Cataloguing in Publication data available

Library of Congress Cataloging-in-Publication data
Chandler, Rachel, 1982-
The most important lessons in life : letters to a young girl / by
Rachel Chandler.
p. cm.
Originally published: Garden City, N.Y. : Guild America Books,
1997.
ISBN 1-86204-420-1 (alk. paper)
1. Conduct of life. 2. Celebrities– Correspondence. 3. Chandler,
Rachel, 1982- . I. Title
BJ1581.2.C268 1998
170'.44–dc21   98-24918   CIP

Printed in Hong Kong through Worldprint

ISBN 1-86204-420-1

I dedicate this
book to
My Family
for their
help and
encouragement

Introduction

I was so nervous that I couldn't sleep. It was the night before the interview and all I could think about were the cameras, the lights, and the millions of people watching me. Then I remembered what Lily Tomlin had written in her letter to me. I turned to it in my large scrapbook and read her words: "One thing of importance that I can tell you: 'The human mind cannot hold two opposing thoughts at the same time.' So, if you hold a positive thought, you cannot hold a negative one."

So I began to think of all the positive thoughts and advice given to me from people all over the world. I flipped through the hundreds of letters I had received:

The words from Mother Teresa, writing from the slums of India: "[Be] the sunshine of God's love." And Whoopi Goldberg's advice: "Be true to yourself. The rest will fall into place."

"You can do or be anything if you work hard," written by John Mellencamp. Barbara Bush's letter, saying, "You have special talents and abilities, and you can make a difference for the better . . ."

But wait—you may wonder how an eleven-year-old girl from a small town in Virginia could have such famous pen pals.

Well, it all began one wintry week in 1993 when we were out of school because of icy weather. I asked my dad and mom what they thought was the most important lesson they'd learned in their lives. My dad said it was to persevere, to keep trying and not give up. My mom said that she had learned that family was the most important part of her life.

My dad suggested I write to famous people I respected or admired to seek their responses. My mom thought that if I wrote to famous women, I could use this information for a Girl Scouts project that my junior troop was working on at the time, a badge about women's careers. One requirement was to interview women who were in jobs or careers that are usually dominated by men. So I decided to write to several famous women and see what they felt was the reason for their success or was the most important lesson that they had learned in their lives. As I became more excited about the project, I decided to add to my list prominent men, too.

So during the winter ice storms of that year, I sat at our computer and typed out many, many letters. I sent out over two hundred letters to prominent people. In my letter I introduced myself, explained my Girl Scouts project, and wrote what my mom and dad had answered, and I asked what they thought was the most important lesson in their life. My dad and I went to the library and researched the addresses of the people. It was a lot of work, but I enjoyed it.

My parents warned me not to get my hopes up too high, because these were very busy people who might not have time to write back. Also, they explained that many celebrities never actually receive their mail. Their secretaries or office assistants usually open and answer the mail without the celebrity ever seeing it. So I tried to think positively but also planned not to be too disappointed if I didn't receive any answers.

In a couple of months I began to receive answers to my letters—lots of letters, from celebrities, authors, artists, movie stars, and government officials. And they weren't just letters that their secretaries wrote; these were written by the actual people. At first it was hard to believe that these letters were written by famous people who were taking time from their busy schedules to answer my questions.

One of the first letters I received, and one that meant a lot to me, was from Danielle Steel, the best-selling author. I have never read her books, but my mom has and so have millions of other people. Her letter was two typed pages. Dad said it looked like it was typed on an old manual type-writer. In her letter, she said it was late at night and she had just finished her sixtieth book and was going to send it to the publisher. She wanted to answer my letter herself, instead of having someone do it for her.

Ms. Steel wrote that she agreed with my mom that family was very important, and she spoke a little about her own wonderful family. She also said my dad was right to say determination or perseverance was an important lesson to learn. She told me that her first book sold quickly, but her next five manuscripts were all turned down. She said she kept trying until her seventh book sold, and she's been with it ever since. If she had quit trying, she would not be where she is today. She also sent me an autographed book, *The Accident*, but said I had to wait until I was eighteen to read it, if my parents said it was okay. I can hardly wait.

Many other people wrote to me, too. It was exciting to go to the mailbox to see if I had gotten any letters.

Another one of my favorites was the card I mentioned earlier from Mother Teresa. I know she is such a busy and giving person, helping the poor. It made me very thankful that she would take time out to answer the question of a young girl who lived across the world. She said that God loved me and that I should try to be "the sunshine of God's love."

Mr. Cooke, who owns the Washington Redskins football team, wrote a five-page letter. I knew he had taken a lot of time to answer my question. He quoted a lot of famous people and what they felt was the meaning of life. He said that "humanity is divided into three parts: (a) those who make things happen; (b) those who watch things happen; and (c) those who don't know what's happening." He ended by saying that "if you want something more than anyone else in the world wants it, and you're willing to exercise the utmost intelligence and industry to get it, it will be yours."

I wrote to Mikhail Gorbachev in Moscow. He wrote a letter back in Russian. A friend of mine, Alina Lippa, who is Russian, translated it for me. But then we noticed it was printed in English on the back. Mr. Gorbachev said it was good for people my age to think about their future. "The main thing is to respect your own human dignity and to value and respect it in other people."

Archbishop Desmond Tutu of South Africa sent me a picture and his prayers. He stated that to know that God loves you and to believe in yourself is the best advice he could give.

My dad and I placed all of these in a scrapbook and added to them almost every day. I received many letters, from all over the United States and from countries all around the world.

Even though I received so many letters, I was still disappointed that some people didn't respond. I was hoping to hear from the queen of England and Princess Di and several rock stars. But I understood that these were very important and busy people who could not possibly answer all of the thousands of letters they receive, and learning this was a good lesson for me.

One day my dad and I were talking to a reporter, Sarah Huntley, from our hometown paper, the Roanoke Times. During our conversation, she learned about my Girl Scouts project, was very interested in it, and wanted to see the scrapbook. She went back and talked with her editor, and they decided my project would make a good story for the paper. Ms. Huntley and photographer Roger Hart came out to my house and took lots of pictures of me and my letters. Ms. Huntley wrote a wonderful article, and the story ended up on the next day's front page. Boy, was I surprised!

At school that day, my friends and teachers—and even people I didn't know—kept saying, "I saw your picture in the paper." "Way to go!" "Neat idea." "Can you give me the address of Brad Pitt?"

The same day, I was called out of class into Principal Kay Duffy's office. My dad was there and he had some interesting news for me. He told me Mom had received a phone call from the *CBS This Morning* show. The producer of the show had seen my story on the wires of the *Associated Press*. The article had said I was a Girl Scout and the producer had called to the Virginia Girl Scouts office to get the name and phone number of my Girl Scouts leader, who just happened to be my mom. The producer asked Mom if I could fly to New York and be on their show. So when my dad came to school to ask if I would do it, my answer was "YES!" On that same day, the *NBC Today* show's producer called and asked me to be on their show. How exciting!

My dad and I flew to New York days later to be on TV. It was wild. I was so nervous, waiting for the interviews to take place. But all my family and friends said I appeared so calm and I did a good job. Katie Couric interviewed me for the *Today* show, and Mr. Smith interviewed me for *CBS This Morning*.

In the next few weeks I received calls from people at radio and TV stations from all over the world. They interviewed me over the telephone. One lady from Japan called, and our connection was not very good. She was very patient, and I hope I answered all her questions correctly. The BBC of England called, and we talked a long time. The reporter asked about the Queen "Mum" and Princess Di, but I told him that they had not responded to my letters and also that I realized they were very busy. He laughed and said they definitely were busy trying to solve their own problems. (Not too long after this phone interview, I received letters from the ladies-in-waiting for the queen and princess, explaining why they could not answer my letter, but they wished me the best.)

I had interviews with TV stations in Canada. I went to our local TV station, WDBJ, Channel 7, and was interviewed by the Canadian stations via satellite.

Well, just when I thought all the attention was about to fade out and things would get back to normal, I received a phone call from a publishing company. They wanted to take my letters and make them into a book.

Who would have believed that what started out as a requirement for a

Girl Scouts patch would turn into all this? Instead of using the information toward the patch, I used it as my Silver Award Project and presented it to a young Brownie troop in Roanoke. And instead of letters in a personal scrapbook, the best of the letters are here, in this book, which I can share with you.

And what have I learned from all this? I think that each lesson that you learn helps to make you who you are. It is helpful to look at what others have experienced and try to learn from his or her advice. Each person is unique and special, and his or her "most important lesson" is worth listening to—or, as in this case, reading about.

RACHEL CHANDLER

Hello, my name is Rachel Chandler. I live in Roanoke, Virginia. I am 11 years old, and I am in the 7th grade. I have a learning disability, but I work very hard and make the honor roll in school. My dad says that I can do or be anything if I work hard. He says that girls are as smart as boys. I may be a doctor or a writer when I grow up.

What do you think is the most important thing to learn in life? My dad says that I should have determination and my mom says to know the importance of family. I am writing to great people to get advice. I am writing a report for my Girl Scout project and for school.

I see you on TV and you seem so nice and smart. If you ever come to Roanoke you can come by and see us. Thank you for helping me.

Love,

Rachel Chandler

"*I am writing to great people to get advice.*"

Letters

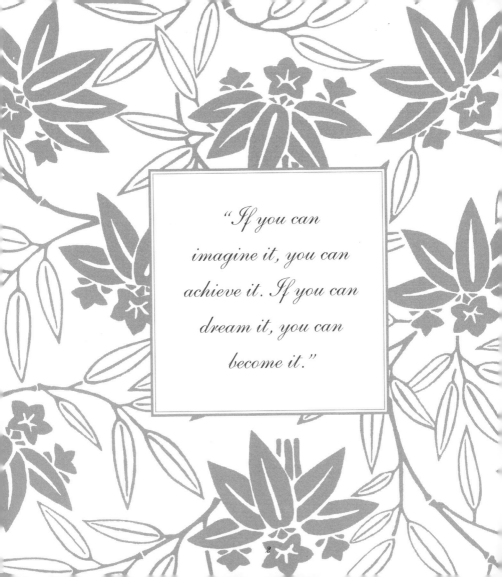

"If you can imagine it, you can achieve it. If you can dream it, you can become it."

DEAR RACHEL,

Thank you for your wonderful letter! I was very touched to hear from you—usually, there is someone who helps me to answer my mail, but I liked your letter so much that I thought I'd answer it myself.

I write mostly at night because that way I can be with my children all day long, which is what I try to do. I pick everyone up at school, and they go to ballet, karate, tennis, computer lessons, and all kinds of stuff. We also have four dogs, a bird, and a black pig (named Coco). This is silly information, since you wrote me a much more serious letter.

I agree with everything your father says. You can do and be anything you want in your life—there are no limitations. I'm not just saying that because it sounds good—I really mean it. There was a wonderful quote when my oldest daughter graduated last year. She's a psychologist. But the quote was, I think, very important. I had it framed and gave it to all my children. This is what it says.

"If you can imagine it, you can achieve it.

 If you can dream it, you can become it."

Think about it, it's a wonderful message.

I also agree with your mom that family is the most important. "Other stuff" fades away, friends are important, but sometimes they change and move on, the people who mean a lot to you now may not mean as much to you later. But your family is the greatest gift you have—especially if you have a nice one, which it sounds like you do. I really treasure my family—they're what's best about my life, and what I love most.

And the best "advice" I can give is about perseverance. Your father called it determination. It's a great thing. With perseverance, you can do anything you want. Just don't give up—you've got to stick with it. When I started writing, I sold my first book very quickly. But after that, no one bought my next five books. For some reason—perseverance, I guess, or just plain stubbornness—I kept on writing, and the 7th book sold and I've been at it ever since. I have written 59 books now, and am just finishing my 60th (tonight, in fact)—think of the career I would have missed if I had stopped writing when those first five books didn't sell. I would never have had the life and career I've had since. Many things would have changed in my life,

4

and not for the better. Perseverance is the greatest thing you can have. Just keep at it!!

You sound like a remarkable young lady, and I wish you happy things. I'm sure you will do something wonderful one day, because you know you can. (A learning disability can't stop you, lots of successful people have them.) I wish you success, and happiness, and a happy life. Thank you for writing to me. It was very special for me.

Love,

Danielle Steel

Author

DEAR RACHEL,

I feel that I am a very lucky man to have the love and respect of such wonderful young people from all over the world.

I think the most important thing to learn in life is how to live with all sorts of people and to make each other happy and content. I think we must all strive to be at peace with ourselves and each other.

Your mum and dad are very lucky to have such a wonderful young daughter, and I am sure you are going to be a doctor or writer one day. Keep working hard and you will achieve.

I am deeply honoured that you wrote to me and I thank you.

With warm wishes to you and your family,

Yours sincerely,

Nelson Mandela

President, African National Congress, Cape Town, South Africa

" . . . we must all strive to be at peace with ourselves and each other."

DEAR RACHEL,

Thanks for your nice letter. Congratulations on making the honor roll.

Having two daughters of my own, I agree with your dad that women can do anything they set their minds to. It just takes perseverance, determination, and hard work. And your mom is right about the importance of family. My own parents were my greatest role models. I am where I am today because of their love, nurturing, and guidance.

Rachel, I'm very proud of you for doing so well in school despite your disability. It just goes to show that we can overcome most obstacles by believing in ourselves and working hard. . . .

Sincerely,

Colin Powell

General, U.S. Army (Ret.)

"...perseverance, determination, and hard work."

DEAR RACHEL,

Thank you for your kind letter. I'm always glad to get to know my television friends in a real way through the mail. You told me that you have a learning disability and that you work hard and that you make the honor roll at school. Even though you may have some difficulties, it's wonderful to know that you have found ways to learn and to succeed. Working hard is certainly an important part of that. I'm proud of the many ways you're learning and growing, and I hope you are, too.

You also told me that you are writing a report for Girl Scouts and for school about the most important thing to learn in life. It was interesting to know your parents' thoughts about that. You are fortunate to have parents who care so much about family and about determination. I'm honored that you'd like me to be a part of your project. I think the most important thing in life to understand is that every human being has value, and that we all have some struggles and challenges that we're meeting as well as we can. That's the basis for all healthy relationships, and it's through relationships that we grow and learn best. That's been an important foundation for our Neighborhood programs and for my own life.

Best wishes from all of us here in the Neighborhood for whatever you do. You are special—just because you're you!

Sincerely,

Fred Rogers

Host of Mr. Rogers' Neighborhood

Dear Rachel,

Rachel, both of your parents are right.

Always do your best!

SINCERELY,

CLARENCE THOMAS

JUSTICE, UNITED STATES SUPREME COURT

DEAR RACHEL,

Thank you for your letter. . . . I have an eleven-year-old son who is a sixth grader, and also I have a nine-year-old daughter.

There are many important lessons to learn in life. Treating other people with love and respect is the most important, in my opinion. Hard work, determination, and perseverance are necessary for success in any endeavor or career. Service to God and family is the only true way to happiness.

I could go on, but I think that's enough. Best of luck to you.

Sincerely,

John Grisham

Author

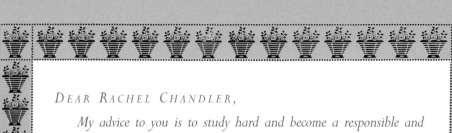

Dear Rachel Chandler,

My advice to you is to study hard and become a responsible and caring citizen. You have special talents and abilities, and you can make a difference for the better—at home, at school, in your place of worship, and in your community. Becoming involved in these areas is an important first step toward building a better America.

Continue to work hard in school because your education is invaluable. You should never forget how important good reading and thinking skills are. From the time I was your age I have read constantly and encourage you to do the same. Reading has opened a world to me and keeps me open to the world, and I wish the same for you.

Best wishes for a successful future.

Warmly,

Barbara Bush,

Former First Lady

DEAR RACHEL CHANDLER,

Thank you for your letter. Jesus loves you in a very special way. He has given you lots of joy and love, in order to share with others. You too can do to Jesus little acts of love in the poor, lonely, and the neglected ones of your city. God loves you and asks that you share this love with all you meet. Today be the sunshine of God's love to your parents, friends, and neighbors. Keep the joy of loving God in your heart, and share this joy with all.

God bless you.

Mother Teresa

Founder, Missionaries of Charity

Calcutta, India

DEAR RACHEL,

Your dad is absolutely right. You can be whatever you want provided you are prepared to make a commitment to work as hard as is necessary to achieve your aim.

The fact that you have a learning problem does not bar you from being successful. It does mean, however, that you probably have to work two or three times harder than those children who do not have a learning disability. Those of us who are LD learn differently, and because people don't really know how best to teach us, it takes us much longer to learn.

I think that the most important thing is to choose a career that you know you will enjoy working at. That way work is fun and learning becomes so much easier. Once you have started to be successful I think you will find that you continue on to do extremely well. LD people who are successful usually have a high work ethic. We learned at a young age how to work hard, and that stays with us. Those who found learning easy have often not ever had to struggle and therefore do not have the same long-term determination.

Choose what you want to do. Give your all to it and practice, practice, practice it.

I wish you every success.

Sincerely,

P. Buckley Moss

Artist

"*Don't create barriers for yourselves or put limits on your aspirations . . .*"

Dear Rachel,

Many times I am asked by young people how I have achieved my success as an actress. Here are some thoughts that have certainly been part of my master plan for success. As an almost completely self-educated woman (I left school when I was 12!) I know how important it is to avail yourself of what is there for each and every one of you if only you use these precious years of education to your advantage.

Don't create barriers for yourselves or put limits on your aspirations— keep stretching and enlarging your mind so that you can envision participating in life in more exciting and meaningful ways— Let's face it, there are no restrictions in this country of ours as to what you can achieve with education, if you believe you can. If you use your energy in positive and productive ways, you can hope to achieve your dreams. On the other hand, when we use that energy in negative ways it will undoubtedly produce a negative result and disappointment. Expose yourself to every bit of information past, present, and future to enhance your intelligence. . . .

Our time at school is spent with books, mainly textbooks, which often

become a drag to read because they only offer facts about a given subject—
On the other hand, books of fiction and nonfiction are an entertainment
unto themselves. Do yourself a favor and turn off the television on occasion
and sink into the wonderful world of a really good story. How about a mystery? The first book I read when I was about ten years old was National Velvet, which was a best-seller in 1935 by Enid Bagnold. I was transported by
this vivid story of a young girl with a passion for a horse called "Pie," whom
she believed could win the great steeplechase in England called the Grand
National (talk about believing in yourself!). I certainly never dreamed that
ten years later I would appear in that movie playing Velvet's sister Edwina!

I love the story of Jonathan Livingston Seagull. It appeals to my personal belief that if you aspire to succeed in life beyond what appears to be
your limitations, you can fly higher and longer than those around you. Visualize yourself succeeding in your chosen field.

Don't be afraid to be different—the greatest success stories are those
about people who defied the tendency to just run with the crowd.

You'll never know what you're good at in life if you don't experiment with ideas— Reach out to new sources of inspiration— Learn a subject you know nothing about. Listen to music—all music. Grow a garden. Learn to cook! Volunteer, read the newspaper. Learn a language. Take up a sport. But whatever it is you finally end up doing, enjoy your work knowing you do it really well—whether it be a building maintenance person or a professor of chemistry!

GOOD LUCK!

Angela Lansbury

Actress

Рэчел Чендлер
Ранок, Вирджиния
США

Дорогая Рэчел!

Большое спасибо за твое письмо. Очень хорошо, когда люди уже в таком возрасте задумываются о своем будущем.

Ты пишешь, что хочешь стать врачом или писателем. Это хорошие и нужные профессии. Врач лечит человека от болезней, а настоящий писатель может вылечить человеческую душу. На свете существуют много нужных и полезных профессий и дел. Разве плохо быть доброй супругой и заботливой матерью? Видимо, главное состоит в том, чтобы быть полезным другим людям, своей стране, обществу. Главное - уважать человеческое достоинство в себе и ценить и уважать его в других людях.

Поэтому хочу пожелать тебе успехов на любом поприще, которое ты изберешь для себя. Передай от меня привет твоим папе и маме.

С уважением.

Михаил Горбачев

DEAR RACHEL,

Thank you for your letter. It is so good when people of your age think about their future.

You are writing you want to become a doctor or a writer. These are good and necessary professions. A doctor cures people of diseases and a writer can cure people's souls. There are many necessary and useful professions and endeavours in the world. Is it not good to become a good wife and a caring mother? The main thing, as it seems, is to be useful to other people, your nation, and society. The main thing is to respect your own human dignity and to value and respect it in other people.

So I wish you success in any capacity that you may choose. Give my regards to your mom and dad.

Respectfully,

Mikhail Gorbachev

Former President of the U.S.S.R.

" . . . to respect your own human dignity and to value and respect it in other people."

DEAR MISS CHANDLER,

Her Royal Highness has asked me to tell you that she has a list in answer to your question! It is as follows: to give to others; a moment's kindness and a smile can mean the world; give people respect and dignity by listening; try and find the best in people; forgiveness. . . .

Her Royal Highness has asked me to convey her best wishes and thank you for thinking of her.

Yours sincerely,

The Office of Sarah Ferguson,
Duchess of York

Dear Ms. Chandler,

WHAT A WONDERFUL LETTER, YOU CERTAINLY SOUND LIKE A NICE YOUNG LADY. YOU ARE EXTREMELY FORTUNATE TO HAVE ONDERFUL PARENTS WHO CAN OFFER SUCH GREAT ADVICE. TO ANSWER YOUR QUESTION ABOUT THE MOST IMPORTANT THINGS IN LIFE, I AGREE WITH YOUR PARENTS THAT YOU NEED DETERMINATION AND TO HAVE THE SUPPORT OF YOUR FAMILY. AS LONG AS YOU MAINTAIN THOSE STRENGTHS AND KEEP YOUR GOALS IN SIGHT, LIFE WILL BE FINE. . . .

SINCERELY,
JOHN D. (JAY) ROCKEFELLER IV
UNITED STATES SENATOR (WEST VIRGINIA)

"*Do what you believe is right.*"

DEAR RACHEL:

The most important lesson you may ever learn is to realize the importance and value of love for yourself, as well as for others—no matter how different or difficult you or they may be. I'm talking about the kind of love that seeks what is best for the individual, not what sometimes passes for love.

To do this:

1. Know that you are a child of God, valuable and unique. You were created to fill your own special niche . . . it may be large or it may be small. I believe this is true for everyone.

2. Be honest about weaknesses in yourself and others. Deal with them the best you can, but focus on positive qualities—they are there.

3. After getting the facts, think a situation through, then act in love. Do what you believe is right. You have to live with yourself, so avoid doing anything that would make you lose love or respect for yourself. Shakespeare said, "This above all: to thine own self be true, And it must follow, as the night the day, Thou canst not then be false to any man."

Best wishes!

Lillien S. Brown, Ed.D.

School Psychologist (Retired)

DEAR RACHEL,

These are such exciting times we live in, and my most important lesson has been to understand that a positive and productive life is up to each one of us individually.

We are our own realizers. We are our own best teachers.

Remember to keep the knowingness that the God source is within you. Trust it and your life and love will reflect it!

Much love,

Shirley MacLaine

Actress

DEAR RACHEL:

It is obvious from your letter that you already know the most important lessons of life. Your determination to succeed is clear evidence of that.

Both your mother and dad have given you very good advice because, while it is difficult to achieve a good balance in life, it is critically important. Perhaps one good thing to remember is that luck is when opportunity meets preparedness. If you don't work hard and if you are not prepared, you will never be able to take advantage of the opportunities life gives you. Obviously, that will not be a problem for you.

Your dad was right when he said girls are as smart as boys, and you certainly can do anything you choose to do or be anything you choose to be. . . .

Yours sincerely,

Christine Todd Whitman

Governor of New Jersey

DEAR RACHEL:

It is good to see a young lady such as yourself take an active interest in the question "What is the most important thing to learn in life?" I believe that the advice your mother and father gave you about this question will serve you well in life. If you pursue all of your goals with determination and always remember the importance of family, you will be well on the way toward success in all your future pursuits.

In addition to these important lessons, I believe your report should stress the importance of personal responsibility and civic duty. Unfortunately, men and women too often forget these basic principles of good citizenship. Throughout your life, if you consistently take responsibility for your actions, you will develop a strength of character that will make you a leader among your peers. As a leader, others will look to your example. Such responsibility must not be taken lightly. Embrace it with vigor. As a responsible and respected member of the community, you will be expected to promote admirable virtues—honesty, kindness, and charity. These important qualities will help you to live up to your civic duty of service to your fellow man. . . .

With warm regards, I remain,

Sincerely,

George Allen

Governor of Virginia

Dear Rachel,

In answer to your question

{Archbishop Tutu} believes that to know that

God loves you and to believe in yourself

is the best advice he can give you.

YOURS SINCERELY,

THE OFFICE OF THE MOST REVEREND DESMOND TUTU,

ANGLICAN ARCHBISHOP OF CAPE TOWN, SOUTH AFRICA

DEAR RACHEL,

Congratulations on making the honor roll in school; there is obviously not much advice I can give you because you seem to be on the right track. I think your dad is right: if you work hard, dedicate yourself, and fulfill your potential with the support of a good family around, you will succeed. . . .

Best wishes,

Greg Norman

Professional Golfer

DEAR MISS CHANDLER,

President Havel greatly admires your strength and perseverance in working hard to overcome your learning disability. Both your parents are right in what they say. One of the most important things to learn in life is to be yourself and believe in yourself.

The President thanks you once again for your letter, and sends you his warmest greetings. Keep up the wonderful attitude!

Sincerely,

The Office of Václav Havel,
President of the Czech Republic

". . . be yourself and believe in yourself."

DEAR RACHEL,

I am so sorry that we did not meet when you were in New York, but thank you for taking time to write to me.

Enclosed is a personally autographed picture for your best friend, Megan, and one for you, too.

In your letter you asked what is the most important lesson in life to learn. Observe the Lord's Commandments and everything else will fall into place.

Keep well, Rachel. Love,

Willard Scott

The Today Show

"Observe the Lord's Commandments and everything else will fall into place."

DEAR RACHEL:

You've asked a tough question! There are many important things to learn. I've found I can only learn by one incident at a time. Each day learn a little from the encounters that cross your path. Consider this incident:

It was Christmas 1962. I was twelve. My father gave my two brothers and myself a BB gun, along with detailed lessons on safety. That Christmas we made a trip to my grandmother Ellcessor. We arrived fully armed. Three boys with BB guns. Behind Nana's house was a large field that contained what appeared to be a dumping ground for old vehicles. We loaded the front windshield of an old Jeep with enough BBs to sink a ship. Little did we know that this was a recycling yard where a person could take usable parts from one vehicle to restore others. I remember that incident because I lost my gun for a long time. I lost it because I had not yet learned several lessons.

It's often said that experience is a great teacher. I found this to be the truth. So learn from your experiences. Learn from those that you may for the moment call "bad." If the truth be known, they can all be good.

If my faith means anything, it means God always gives us a second chance. If we fall down, we can get up again. This is not just humans "picking themselves up by their own bootstraps." It's a sense that something bigger than ourselves is at work in this world. The kind of God we create or follow has a lot to do with how we view ourselves and how we treat others.

Rachel Chandler has a great heritage. You are blessed to have a mom and dad like RoJane and Michael. You are also blessed to have a brother like Aaron. But they are blessed to have someone named Rachel. Protect your name. It tells the world who you are and where you come from. And if you must sacrifice your reputation, go ahead. Only make sure it's worthy of the sacrifice. Only experience can teach you the wisdom of that choice.

Your Pastor,

Gregory L. Adkins

Pastor, Raleigh Court United Methodist Church

DEAR RACHEL:

The most important thing to learn in life is that one should never give up: every problem can be addressed and, if not eliminated, reduced in adverse impact.

Your mom is absolutely right when she says, "Know the importance of family." When things are tough and when things are terrific, it is wonderful to have your family either supporting or celebrating.

You were nice to write. In the event I am ever in Roanoke, I will certainly call you.

All the best.

Sincerely,

Edward I. Koch

Former Mayor of New York City

Dear Rachel:

ONE THING OF IMPORTANCE THAT I CAN TELL YOU:

"THE HUMAN MIND CANNOT HOLD TWO OPPOSING THOUGHTS AT

THE SAME TIME." SO, IF YOU HOLD A POSITIVE THOUGHT,

YOU CANNOT HOLD A NEGATIVE ONE.

WITH LOVE,

LILY TOMLIN

ACTRESS

*"Funny thing,
the harder I work
the luckier I get."*

DEAR MS. CHANDLER,

I regret I cannot come up with an easy, simple recipe for success, since I believe there's no surefire method of reaching the top. But for starters I believe that humanity is divided into three parts:

(a) Those who make things happen,
(b) Those who watch things happen, and
(c) Those who don't know what's happening.

In the course of my life I've run across maxims that seem to relate to success. But don't forget that success frequently is a state of mind rather than a material pinnacle.

So, here are a few of those thoughts I have found helpful:

GLORY

". . . a man's reach should exceed his grasp, Or what's a heaven for?"
　　—Robert Browning

"It ain't bragging if ya done it."　—Dizzy Dean

COURAGE

"I am a little hurt but I am not slain
I will lay me down for to bleed a while
Then I'll rise and fight with you again."

>—John Dryden

LUCK

"Luck is the residue of design."   —Branch Rickey

"Funny thing, the harder I work the luckier I get."

>—Lord Thomson of Fleet

"Be grateful for luck. Pay the thunder no mind—listen to the birds.
And don't hate nobody."   —Eubie Blake

"Fortune smiles on the man who is prepared."   —Louis Pasteur

PRACTICE VS. THEORY

"Some Greeks had been sitting on a wall for over a week theorizing
which would fall first, a feather or a pellet of lead of the
same weight.

"A Roman came along, listened for a few minutes, and said,

'For God's sake, drop them and find out.'"   —Anonymous

PREPAREDNESS

Said he owed his success to "being there five minutes ahead
of the other chaps."   —Admiral Horatio Nelson

INTUITION

"That which is essential cannot be seen with the eye. Only with
the heart can one know it rightly."   —The Bible

THE FUTURE

"Things without all remedy should be without regard.
What's done is done."   —Shakespeare

DETERMINATION

(a) "It is no use saying, 'We are doing our best.' You have got
to succeed in doing what is necessary."
(b) "Never talk to the monkey when the organ grinder is in the room."
—Winston Churchill

"Out of the night that covers me,
Black as the Pit from pole to pole,
I thank whatever gods may be
For my unconquerable soul."

—William Ernest Henley

ENERGY

"Enthusiasm is akin to genius."   —Anonymous

AGE

(a) "How old would you be if you didn't know how old you were?"

(b) "Age is a matter of mind over matter. If you don't mind,
it doesn't matter."   —Satchel Paige

ALL THE RULES ROLLED INTO ONE

(a) "Avoid fried meats, which angry up the blood."

(b) "Avoid running at all times. Don't look back.
Something might be gaining on you."

—Satchel Paige

"Every sickness ain't death,

And every good-bye ain't gone."

  —Carl Rowan

(a) "Humility is the most difficult of all virtues to achieve."

(b) "Nothing dies harder than the desire to think well of oneself."

  —T. S. Eliot

I can only add that it has always seemed to me that if you want something more than anyone else in the world wants it, and that if you're willing to exercise the utmost intelligence and industry to get it, it will be yours.

Best wishes for success.

Yours very truly,

Jack Kent Cooke

Owner, Washington Redskins

DEAR MS. CHANDLER:

My advice is to stick to it—whatever the "it" is . . . a team sport, a tough calculus problem, or a job that might become a career. You don't have to know right now exactly where you're heading or what you'll be. . . . But when you do know, go after it and don't lose sight of your goal. . . .

Sincerely,

The Office of William Weld
Governor of Massachusetts

DEAR RACHEL:

It sounds like you are getting good advice from your parents. Your learning disability will hinder you only if you let it. Did you know that one of our greatest minds had a learning disability? He was Albert Einstein. Celebrities such as Cher and Tom Cruise are success stories and have had to cope with a learning disability. Just remember, hard work always pays off in the end, so keep up the good work in school.

I believe the most important thing to learn in life is to follow the Golden Rule. If we can treat others the way we would like to be treated, the world would be a much better place. As a fellow Girl Scout, good luck on your project!

Sincerely,

Patricia Schroeder

United States Congresswoman (Colorado)

". . . be at peace with

who you are . . ."

DEAR RACHEL,

If I were to choose one thing as the most important idea to learn in life, it would be to believe in yourself and in everything you can be. You are the only person whom you will be with for the rest of your life, so you should learn to be at peace with who you are and how valuable you are in God's eyes. I've known people in my life who had many advantages—had a high intelligence, were born into comfortable and loving families—but when they failed to take stock of how valuable they themselves were, they were very unhappy. When you believe in yourself, not only will you be happy, but you will be able to appreciate the good qualities of the people around you.

Family is also very important, and it sounds to me like you have a supportive and loving one. You are very lucky for that, because a solid foundation that you get from a loving family will give you strength when troubles visit your life. . . .

Best,

James Finn Garner

Actor

To Rachel,

Your dad's right. Girls are as smart as boys. You can do or be anything if you work hard.

JOHN MELLENCAMP

SINGER AND SONGWRITER

DEAR RACHEL:

I believe that both of your parents were correct when they told you that family and perseverance are important values. They have played a vital role in my life. I still depend on the wisdom and support that my parents gave me. . . .

With kind regards, I am

Sincerely,

John Warner

United States Senator (Virginia)

DEAR RACHEL:

Always remember that what is really important to you can be achieved. Sometimes our greatest weaknesses become our greatest strengths. When I was beginning as a public speaker I was so nervous that my knees shook and I fainted. I wanted to be a teacher but was so afraid. Eventually with practice I became a famous speaker.

When I went to school I was not a good writer. When I was 32 years old I decided that I really wanted to be a good writer. With a lot of determination (as your dad recommends) I began writing and eventually wrote a national best-seller [*Men Are from Mars, Women Are from Venus*]. I hope you will hold on to your dreams and be a loving person, and I am sure in your lifetime you will express the beautiful potential you are here to express.

Always remember it is loving family and relationships (as your mother recommends) that provide a solid foundation for a lifetime of success and fulfillment.

Always grow in love.

John Gray

Author and Motivational Speaker

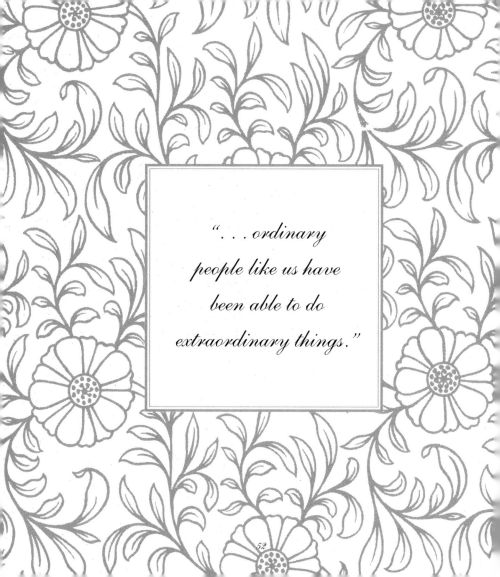

"... ordinary
people like us have
been able to do
extraordinary things."

DEAR RACHEL:

Despite the fact that neither of my parents graduated from high school, my mother decided before I was born that I would go to college someday. I resisted her plan; I failed the third, seventh, and ninth grades, but my mother prodded me every step of the way through high school, through college, and on to a Ph.D. in economics. Not one of my teachers ever imagined that I would one day become a United States Senator.

I like to remind young people like you that America is not a great and powerful country because the most brilliant and talented people in the world come to live here. America is a great and powerful country because it was here that ordinary people like you and me have had more opportunity and more freedom than any other people who have ever lived on the face of the planet. And with that opportunity and that freedom ordinary people like us have been able to do extraordinary things. . . .

Yours respectfully,

Phil Gramm

United States Senator (Texas)

DEAR RACHEL:

It sounds as if you are already getting good advice from your family, but let me explain a few things that I believe are important to learn in one's life.

No matter what adversities you face, don't let them stop your ambitions and dreams. Your father is right. Girls are as smart as boys, and if your goal is to be a doctor or a writer, you can accomplish this goal with hard work and veracity.

Remember, a strong work ethic, honesty, and a sense of family and community will take you far. . . .

Sincerely,

Fred Thompson

United States Senator (Tennessee)

Dear Rachel:

YOUR PARENTS HAVE GIVEN YOU GOOD ADVICE ABOUT

WHAT IS IMPORTANT IN LIFE. IN ADDITION

TO DETERMINATION AND THE IMPORTANCE OF FAMILY,

I THINK IT IS IMPORTANT TO WORK HARD AT SOMETHING

THAT MEANS A GREAT DEAL TO YOU. . . .

SINCERELY,

RICK BOUCHER

UNITED STATES CONGRESSMAN (VIRGINIA)

DEAR RACHEL,

I have four kids of my own (including one named Rachel), so I've thought a lot about what kinds of values to pass along to them. What I've come up with is:

1. Be kind and honest with other people

2. Be kind to yourself

3. Work hard, but give yourself time to relax

4. The family is a precious source of support; between career and family, family comes first. . . .

Sincerely,

Jonathan Kellerman

Author

DEAR RACHEL:

As Mr. Graham has shared in his Crusade ministry all over the world . . . the most important thing in all the world is to know that . . . Jesus loves you. Mr. Graham and the members of his Team have written the enclosed booklet, "Jesus Loves Me!" to help boys and girls, such as yourself, know this wonderful truth. I trust you will find this booklet to be a blessing as you read and study it. . . .

God bless you, Rachel, and thank you for writing and sharing how much you enjoy watching Mr. Graham on television.

Sincerely,

Sterling Huston

Director, North American Ministries,

Billy Graham Evangelical Association

". . . success is nothing without someone to share it with."

Dear Rachel:

Being a good student is so important because, in addition to making excellent grades, you develop the discipline you need for whatever career you choose, whether a doctor or lawyer. Determination, too, is fundamental for success in anything you pursue, something I'm certain you discovered when you made the honor roll. Congratulations!

I must also agree with your dad that having the love and support of a caring family is the most important, for success is nothing without someone to share it with. Rachel, God has already blessed you with everything you need to become one of the "great people in America." Be sure to show your gratitude by keeping up the good work and by helping others. . . .

Sincerely,

Sharon Pratt Kelly
Former Mayor of the District of Columbia

DEAR RACHEL:

I was very pleased to read your letter. You asked me a question that needs a thoughtful answer, and it's hard in a few words to do justice to your question because I find I can't say one word and feel I've answered you properly. That one word or one quality might be "perseverance," but the problem, as you may know, is to learn how to persevere when it seems the situation is hopeless.

Perhaps I would say this to you. It was first proposed by the philosopher Karl Marx. Everything in my life has confirmed the truth of this for me, that no problem ever arises in the world without a solution for that problem already being present in the world. Learning that is, of course, a process and many difficult and tormenting questions come up along the way. But there is always what we might call an answer to solve the problems; we just have to find it.

Knowing that has given me a confidence to not give up on many occurrences when everyone around me told me it was hopeless and indeed the facts staring me in the face told me it was helpless, but I found the answers. Not once and for all time, but in the process of resolving the questions.

My very best wishes to you. I see you are already well on the way.

Many thanks,

Vanessa Redgrave

Actress

Dear Rachel,

Have goals and keep focused!

LILIAN JACKSON BRAUN

AUTHOR

DEAR RACHEL:

I agree with your father that family and believing in yourself are very important cornerstones of life. I also believe that you must never stop dreaming and reaching for the things you want out of life. And dream big! If you believe in yourself and follow your heart, you can do and achieve whatever you want. . . .

All my best for the future!

Sincerely,

Ann Richards

Former Governor of Texas

Dear Rachel,

In answer to your question as to what I think is the most important thing to learn in life, my answer would be to seek the will of God and let Him direct our path. His will is not always what we want, but He often has better things in store for us.

It is important to set goals and with God's help strive to achieve.

I never thought I would be an author. My dream was to be a nurse—but God had other plans for me, and perhaps I have touched many lives through writing that otherwise I may never have reached. My husband and I also were preparing to go into voluntary service, but just before that happened, God called my husband from this life. The year after that my first book was published. I continued writing and traveling around, doing public speaking, thereby making many friends. So you see my plans did not work out, but something much better was given to me to do. . . .

Keep climbing higher, and if a door closes in your path, remember a window will open for another opportunity.

Sincerely,

Mary Borntrager

Author

DEAR RACHEL:

Your parents are very wise in the advice they gave to you. The best piece of advice that I can offer to you today is to study hard and get the most out of your education. Without a good education, I would not be in my position today. I sincerely believe that a good education is the key to success and self-fulfillment. From the letter I received from you it sounds as though you are already heading in that direction, and you should continue on that path. . . .

Sincerely,

Charles S. (Chuck) Robb

United States Senator (Virginia)

Dear Rachel,

You sound like a wonderful person.

Both your parents are right. You can be anything

you want—and have a family to share it with.

MY LOVE TO YOU,

LEE GRANT

ACTRESS

I agree with your dad that hard work and determination can get you very far. Also, a love of family to keep you going and keep you strong!

When I was growing up, I dreamed about becoming a cowgirl, a detective, a spy, a great actress, or a ballerina. Not a dentist, like my father, or a homemaker, like my mother—and certainly not a writer, although I always loved to read. I didn't know anything about writers. It never occurred to me they were regular people and that I could grow up to become one, even though I loved to make up stories inside my head.

I made up stories while I bounced a ball against the side of our house. I made up stories playing with paper dolls. And I made them up while I practiced the piano, by pretending to give piano lessons. I even kept a notebook with the names of my pretend students and how they were doing. I always had an active imagination. But I never wrote down any of my stories. And I never told anyone about them.

When I grew up, my need for storytelling didn't go away. So when my own two children started preschool I began to write, and I've been writing ever since! My characters live inside my head for a long time before I actually start a book about them. Then, they become so real to me, I talk about them at the dinner table as if they are real. Some people consider this weird. But my family understands. . . .

Love,

Judy Blume

Author

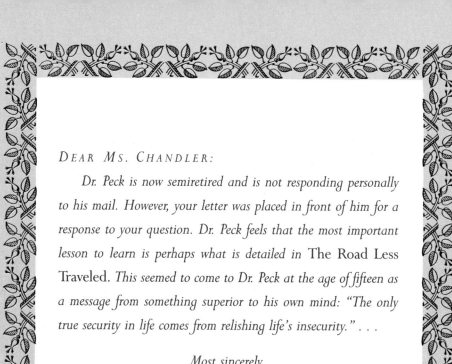

DEAR MS. CHANDLER:

Dr. Peck is now semiretired and is not responding personally to his mail. However, your letter was placed in front of him for a response to your question. Dr. Peck feels that the most important lesson to learn is perhaps what is detailed in The Road Less Traveled. *This seemed to come to Dr. Peck at the age of fifteen as a message from something superior to his own mind: "The only true security in life comes from relishing life's insecurity."* . . .

Most sincerely,

The Office of M. Scott Peck
Author

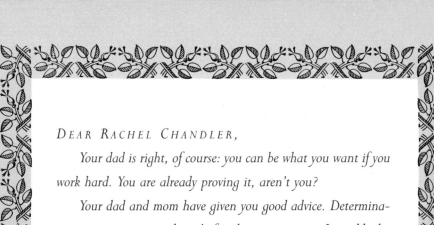

DEAR RACHEL CHANDLER,

Your dad is right, of course: you can be what you want if you work hard. You are already proving it, aren't you?

Your dad and mom have given you good advice. Determination is important, and one's family is important. I would also add that, for me, learning to pay attention to what is actually going on around me is important—and also kindness is important. I am always so touched and grateful when someone is kind to me, takes time to show that they care. So I try to reciprocate! . . .

All best wishes and good luck,

Gail Godwin

Author

Rachel,

I wish I had better answers.

But two very important things in life

are reading and listening!

Good luck—

GOD BLESS,

JOHN GOODMAN

ACTOR

DEAR RACHEL:

My advice to you is: Believe in your ability to do good in the world. Treat everyone with love, even if they don't like you. We are all members of the same family and are here to help each other. I think that is the most important goal of all—much more important and more satisfying than being famous or making money. Those goals don't really bring happiness. But giving your very best to bring happiness to someone else is the most satisfying thing I know to do.

Warmest regards,

Victoria Bond

Former Music Director and Conductor,
Roanoke Symphony Orchestra

DEAR RACHEL:

I agree with your father—girls are just as smart as boys. You have proved that by making the honor roll!

I often hear students say that school does not prepare them for "the real world," and that's not true, either. You are setting goals and then working to achieve them. You are taking information from different sources, evaluating it, and drawing your own conclusions. The most important lesson of all is: Homework never ends. No matter what you decide to do with your life, there will always be something you need to know—about yourself, your job, the world around you.

Young people today face many more challenges than my generation did. I grew up in simpler times. . . . Your generation will also have many more opportunities than mine, and you owe it to yourself to be ready for them. Have the courage of your convictions and take to heart the advice of Amelia Earhart, a Kansan who set many records in aviation's early days: "Everyone has her own Atlantic to fly. Whatever you want very much to do, against the opposition of tradition, neighborhood opposition, and so-called common sense—that is an Atlantic."

Warmest regards,

Nancy Landon Kassebaum
Former United States Senator (Kansas)

DEAR RACHEL:

In the past month I have frequently thought about your question: "What do you think is the most important thing to learn in life?" Every time I ask myself that question I get a different answer. When I ask myself that question I notice that something very interesting happens: I reflect, or reminisce, or become curious, or discover something about myself. Each time I ask myself your question something happens that's a little bit different from the last time I asked myself the question. With that in mind, here is how I choose to answer your question today. . . .

Today . . . I think the most important thing to learn is to look at life as a process. It's more important to look at life as a process of learning, experiencing, and growing than to "grade" ourselves on how successful we are, or how rich we are, how attractive we are, etc. I guess this answer is best summed up in that old saying: "It's not whether you win or lose, but how you play the game." Focusing on the process allows me to think of life as an "adventure" and helps me see beyond current disappointments and setbacks.

My husband and I heard this philosophy articulated about 20 years ago when we were hiking in the "backcountry" of the Smoky Mountains. The trail we took that day was quite isolated and poorly marked. We got lost a few times and had to backtrack. The trail wove back and forth across a river. All totaled, we crossed that river 13 times that day. We crossed it over logs, we crossed it by hopping on rocks, we waded across it after taking our boots off, we sloshed across it with our boots on . . . Each time we crossed it we assumed we wouldn't be crossing it again. Toward the end of the day, as we were getting ready to make camp, a ranger came along and asked us how our day had been.

"The trail is not well marked," we said.

"Yup, that's the adventure," he answered.

"We got lost a couple of times," we continued.

"Yup, that's the adventure," he said again.

"You know, we crossed that river 13 times today."

"Yup, that's the adventure," he concluded.

Eventually, it dawned on us: there probably were many ways to get from point A to point B. . . . If the hike had been a test of how to efficiently travel between two points, we would have "failed." However, in the process of getting back and forth across the river, we had had a great day full of "adventure."

Your letter-writing project provides another example of the importance of process. I think the fact that you are asking the question is more important than the question itself or its answers. I imagine that in the process of asking the question you are learning many things and have experienced a few "adventures." I'll bet that the important lessons are those that you have learned by going through this process. You will get many interesting responses from others, but what is most interesting to me is the impact that doing the project has had on you . . . and on the people you have engaged with your questions. . . .

Sincerely,

Stephanie Pratola

Child Psychologist

DEAR MS. CHANDLER:

Education is very important, and I am sure that with your hard work and diligence, you will . . . become an even better student.

Your parents have provided you with very good advice, and I am certain they will help you set your priorities for your future. . . .

Sincerely,

Barbara Boxer

United States Senator (California)

DEAR RACHEL,

I certainly think that both your mom and dad are correct. With that in mind, I think it is important to set your priorities and stick with them!

From the letter, you seem to be a young lady who will have no trouble overcoming obstacles in your life. I wish you success in what you go after, but mostly I wish you happiness!

With every good wish I remain,

Ralph Emery

Host of The Ralph Emery Show

"... learn how to believe
in yourself."

DEAR RACHEL,

Thank you for your very charming letter.

There are many important lessons in life, and I think your parents named two that are at the top of the list. Since you've called on me to name another one, though, I'd add that I think it's extremely important to learn how to believe in yourself. If you have faith that you can accomplish something, and if you really want to accomplish it, then you will, regardless of your limitations (which we all have, by the way!).

Though I don't get to Virginia too often, it was sweet of you to invite me to visit you. Good luck with your project!

Sincerely,

David Geffen

Record and Film Producer

Rachel,

Be true to yourself.

The rest will fall in place.

WHOOPI GOLDBERG

ACTRESS

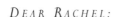DEAR RACHEL:

Your parents have given you grand advice. I agree. Work hard, and don't ever stop trying. You will someday see dreams come true.

Did you know that some of the world's greatest people, including the genius Albert Einstein, had learning disabilities?

With every good wish to you,

Ruth Bader Ginsburg

Justice, United States Supreme Court

DEAR RACHEL:

I agree wholeheartedly with your dad: girls are every bit as smart as boys (and, at times, smarter). There is no limit to what you can achieve in the way of a career if you set goals for yourself and do the hard work that will be required to achieve them.

I would agree with both your parents as to what are the most important things to learn in life. Determination, as your dad has told you, is essential to reaching success. And the warmth and support of a family are equally as important. Judging from what you say about your mom and dad, you live in a wonderful family environment that is full of mutual love and support. . . .

With kindest regards,

Jesse Helms

United States Senator (North Carolina)

DEAR RACHEL:

One of the most important responsibilities of citizens of the United States is to vote on local, state, and federal elections. Though you may not be old enough to vote, you are never too young to begin to educate yourself in preparation for this most important privilege, right, and obligation.

In my opinion, the best preparation for voting is to become a strong student and a skilled researcher. . . . By developing an inquiring mind and using it to sift through information thoroughly, while organizing knowledge in an objective fashion, one maximizes decision-making opportunities. . . .

I deeply appreciate your consulting me for my opinion. I hope that these thoughts will be helpful to you, and I wish you the best with your continued studies.

Sincerely,

Richard G. (Dick) Lugar

United States Senator (Indiana)

DEAR RACHEL:

It's hard to single out the most important thing to learn in life, but let's start with what we all want: a productive, zestful, and challenging adulthood. To achieve this requires commitment and effort, out of which will come some insights that are very useful. (1) You learn there is no reason to hate anybody. (It's not inappropriate to hate certain conditions and actions, but we don't have to hate any humans.) (2) It is desirable to take responsibility for your own actions and health status and not blame other people or external circumstances for your situation in life. . . . (3) And you finally learn what you say your mother stressed: the importance of family. Oddly, when we are little we feel family to be very important. Then as we enter our teens we begin to stress independence, and the importance of family fades. But on becoming mature, we realize again, with far greater insight, that family is the most important thing in the world.

Maybe the most important of these three things to learn in life is the first. If, in maturing, we get rid of all hate, the other things tend to fall into place. Then you mature enough that even old age is not scary. . . .

I wish you a productive, zestful, and challenging life. As a by-product, happiness will inevitably follow.

Sincerely,

Hugh Downs

Broadcast Journalist

DEAR RACHEL:

Rachel, at age 11, the most important thing for you to learn is to take full advantage of your educational opportunities, because after your schooling, you will find that a solid education has given you a wonderful training for your years in later life.

In addition to the foregoing, good character and consideration of others are of great significance, and as you get a little older, think about quality of citizenship and respect for others. . . .

With all good wishes.

Most sincerely,

Walter Annenberg

Philanthropist, Diplomat, Publisher

Dear Miss Chandler:

I AGREE WITH YOUR PARENTS THAT FAMILY

AND DETERMINATION ARE VERY IMPORTANT THINGS IN LIFE.

LEARNING THE IMPORTANCE OF THESE THINGS AT SUCH

A YOUNG AGE IS ADMIRABLE, AND YOU ARE TRULY BLESSED

TO HAVE PARENTS WHO TEACH YOU SUCH VALUES.

I ALSO BELIEVE THAT HONESTY AND COMMITMENT ARE VERY

IMPORTANT THINGS TO LEARN. SETTING GOALS AND THEN

STICKING TO THEM WILL HELP YOU GO FAR IN LIFE. . . .

SINCERELY,

BOB GOODLATTE

UNITED STATES CONGRESSMAN (VIRGINIA)

DEAR RACHEL,

I believe that one of the most important things to learn in life is that you can make a difference in your community no matter who you are or where you live. I have seen so many good deeds—people helped, lives improved—because someone cared. Do what you can to show you care about other people, and you will make our world a better place.

With my best wishes to you and your family,

Sincerely,

Rosalynn Carter

Former First Lady

". . . make a difference in your community . . ."

DEAR RACHEL:

I'm flattered that you came to me for advice. I think it is important to learn as much as you can about everything around you. I truly believe that knowledge is the key to being successful in life. Thus, I feel it is necessary for you to put your best effort into your studies and all of your assignments! If you make it a habit to do that now, when you go on to college and your first job, life will be that much easier! No major adjustments will be needed! A good way to know what's going on around the nation is by reading. For me as a journalist, it's almost impossible to do an interview or ask good questions without being informed by newspapers, magazines, and books. . . .

Sincerely,

Connie Chung

Broadcast Journalist

". . . knowledge
is the key
to being
successful . . ."

DEAR RACHEL,

What challenges you do give! Your question about the lessons I have learned in life really translates into what makes life fulfilling for me, or others. Thankfully, we are all different, so what may bring happiness for me may be another person's burden. However, I do believe that there are some "life traits" that may be applicable to all. Two of these traits are "exercise" and wise decision making.

I believe that for a person to be healthy and happy, all spheres of his life must be exercised. Many exercise the body, many exercise the intellect, some exercise the spirit, and some exercise the emotions. To be balanced, I believe, one must exercise each aspect of the whole person regularly. If any aspect of the whole person is left unstimulated (unexercised), then the person cannot be truly whole. So often we dedicate all of our energies to one aspect of our whole person while the others suffer neglect. A well-weighed balance must be reached to achieve a fulfilling life.

Each day we are faced with many decisions. Some are very simple, like what are we going to wear; others are more complex. . . . On the high end of the scale of important decisions are decisions of a mate or the decision of a life's work. Here much more thought and time are needed. With these decisions, take your time, ask for advice, and "test the waters."

So, in my opinion, the secrets to a fulfilling life are regular exercise in all spheres of one's life, without any areas being left out, and good decision making. By the fact that you have merely asked the question, I have no doubt you will have a fulfilling life. Best of luck.

Sincerely,

Dan Camden, M.D.

Internist

DEAR RACHEL:

Both your mom and dad are absolutely right. You can do anything you decide to do, if you're willing to work hard. You obviously are ready to do that. I have always enjoyed being a writer, but to be a doctor is an excellent goal and allows you to help people more directly.

I'm not sure what the most important thing is that we should learn. It may be a little different for each person. Certainly, family has to be right near the top. For me, the most important thing I had to learn was faith.

Sincerely,

Terry Anderson

Motivational Speaker

Dear Rachel:

IT'S GREAT THAT YOU STUDY AND WORK TOWARD

WHAT YOU WANT. YOUR MOM AND DAD ARE RIGHT. . . .

I THINK IT'S IMPORTANT TO LEARN "YOURSELF." THE MORE

YOU KNOW ABOUT WHY YOU ARE THE WAY YOU ARE, THE

EASIER IT IS TO BE THE PERSON YOU WANT TO BE.

GOOD LUCK!

ADRIENNE BARBEAU

ACTRESS

DEAR RACHEL:

It is I who should learn from you. Perseverance is indeed a worthy trait, and since you already have the gift I won't bother selling you on it.

What I will advise is creativity. Always use your mind for creating visions of ideas, projects, inventions, stories, even reports, or if you wish to be a doctor, creative new methods of medicine. Create at night when you're in bed, create when you look at a flower or a cloud.

I envy you. I was not a good student at school. But I did stare out the window and create dreams, never imagining I was educating myself to someday become a writer of fiction.

I wish you all the best.

Your pal,

Clive Cussler

Author

DEAR RACHEL:

Your parents are correct when they said you could be anything you want to be. Girls and boys are equal, and both are afforded the same skills to use in pursuit of their dreams. The most important thing in life varies for each individual. I agree with your mother that family is extremely important. Family is the backbone of life, and I am thankful for having such a loving and caring family, as I am sure you are. Perseverance, however, is also extremely important because it builds integrity and strengthens an individual's resolve.

These two traits combined will help you lead a happy and successful life. . . .

Sincerely,

Edward M. (Ted) Kennedy

United States Senator (Massachusetts)

Dear Rachel:

[Your] question about what is most important is a good one. Sometimes the best questions are the hardest to answer.

Actually, both your parents are right. Your father is absolutely on target that work ethic can determine your future. It's the advice I give my kids. Set your sights high.

Your mother's belief in the value of family is also right. My wife, Linda, and my three children, Kelly, Lindsey, and Nathan, are the most important people in my life. Their support and love has helped me to achieve my professional goals.

However, dividing time between work and family need not be an either/or decision. Both of your parents are right. You can work very hard in your career and enjoy what you do, but if you don't have family to share your achievements with, your success may seem empty. Family is very important because it sustains us in the tough times and in the work we do.

Rachel, thank you for writing. You made me think about what's truly important in life, and for that, I thank you.

With best wishes, I am

Sincerely,

Tom Daschle

United States Senator (South Dakota)

DEAR RACHEL:

You asked, "What do you think is the most important thing to learn in life?" It sure is difficult to think of one thing. The advice your parents gave you is great. I often say to people to remember that "one person can make a difference." I have certainly found that to be true in my life.

Keep up the good and hard work, Rachel. Stay safe, and God bless you.

Sincerely,

John Walsh

Host of America's Most Wanted

"... *one person can make a difference.*"

DEAR RACHEL:

I believe your parents are right on target with regard to portentous things to learn in life. The significance of family and determination are probably the two most important. However, making a difference in others' lives is also notable. I have devoted my life to making a positive difference in the lives of all Americans through legislation. You must find those things that are meaningful to you and decide how to use them in order to change the lives of others for the better. . . .

Sincerely,

Kweisi Mfume

United States Congressman (Maryland)

". . . {make} a difference in others' lives . . ."

DEAR RACHEL:

To answer your question, I think one of the most important things to learn in life is how to make a positive difference in the lives of others. In school and later at work, it is important to think of ways to help others by our efforts. It sometimes takes extra work, but you are good at that and I feel sure that you will help many people as you grow. I wish you much good luck and lots of happy times.

With love,

Elizabeth Dole

President, American Red Cross

Dear Rachel:

REGARDING YOUR QUESTION ABOUT THE MOST
IMPORTANT THING TO LEARN IN LIFE, MY ANSWER WOULD
HAVE TO BE PERSEVERANCE. YOU HAVE TO CONTINUALLY
STRIVE TO HAVE YOUR GOALS COME TRUE. . . .

BEST PERSONAL REGARDS,
ED DEBARTOLO
OWNER, SAN FRANCISCO 49ERS

DEAR RACHEL:

I'm not sure what the most important thing to learn in life is, because I have not yet learned it. But, that said, there are some things that I think are important, and the sooner learned, the better. Honesty and loyalty are two qualities that come quickly to mind; you can rarely go wrong in life if you employ these regularly.

As a writer, perhaps the most critical thing I've learned is how to be observant—not merely of things around me, but of the shapes and sizes of emotions, thoughts, and desires. When I sit down to write a novel, I need to be able to crawl inside the head and heart of every character, whether they are a hero or a heroine or someone whose every action reeks of evil. Unless those characters become real for me, they won't come to life on the pages I'm writing.

I must say, too, that I agree with your mother and father, that family and determination are very important. I am particularly enamored of determination. I would never have finished anything, especially any of my books, were it not for a hard-nosed, disciplined sense of stick-to-itiveness. I think a sense of refusing to be defeated can carry you far in life, help you overcome setbacks and understand mistakes. If you remain strong and positive about yourself, and always eager to keep learning, both in school and outside, then you can become whatever you want in life. . . .

With very best wishes,

John Katzenbach

Author

"Look for
what is good,
and you will
find it."

DEAR RACHEL,

I thought very hard about your question as to what is the most important thing in life. First, I think to care about what is important is pretty special. Not everyone does, especially as young as you are. I think you have made a great start.

But having thought about it for a while, I think to be able to love people is the most important of all. Never grow bitter or mean of heart. Never give up hope. Look for what is good, and you will find it. You will also see that people will strive to live up to what you believe of them, so you will be making them better at the same time. This will make you a great person in the ways that matter most, and last forever.

If you get some good answers from the people you write to, you could make them into a book. Either a doctor or a writer would be fine things to be. (Actually, I have one brother, and he is a doctor, living in Africa.) Whatever you do, good luck with it. I think you will do very well.

Love,

Anne Perry

Author

Index of Contributors
(LISTED ALPHABETICALLY)